# MISS CHARMING'S BOOK
# OF BAR AMUSEMENTS

# MISS CHARMING'S BOOK OF BAR AMUSEMENTS

## by Cheryl Charming

### Illustrations
### by Ty Pollard

Three Rivers Press/New York

Published by Three Rivers Press, New York, New York.
Member of the Crown Publishing Group.
Random House, Inc., New York, Toronto, London, Sydney, Auckland
www.randomhouse.com

THREE RIVERS PRESS is a registered trademark and the Three Rivers
Press colophon is a trademark of Random House, Inc.

Printed in China

*Miss Charming's Book of Bar Amusements* is produced by becker&mayer!,
Kirkland, Washington.
www.beckermayer.com

Book design by Matt Hutnak
Edited by Marcie DiPietro

Library of Congress Cataloging-in-Publication Data is available
upon request.

ISBN 0-609-80508-8

10 9 8 7 6 5 4 3 2 1

First Edition

Author's Note: Some of the tricks included in this book involve the use
of sharp objects, matches, flammable items, and other potentially
dangerous materials. When performing these tricks, please follow all
directions carefully.

I would like to dedicate this book to all
the crazy and wonderful people who
shared their bar tricks with me; to River
for her unwavering patience, love, and
support; to all the very talented people at
becker&mayer!; and most importantly, to
the Source which resides within me.

# TABLE OF CONTENTS

# INTRODUCTION

Nineteen years ago in the Cabaret, a happening little night-club in Little Rock, Arkansas (it was as happening as things get in Little Rock, anyway), a well-known investment banker nicknamed Daddy Jack turned a brandy snifter upside down over a stemless cherry and challenged onlookers to get the cherry out from under the snifter and into a Manhattan—without touching the cherry! This was the first bar trick I ever saw. The solution amazed the crowd, and my fascination with bar amusements began.

It's been bars and tricks for me ever since. (Hey, there are worse ways to make a living!) A couple of my bartending jobs—working on a cruise ship in the Caribbean and at Walt Disney World—exposed me to large volumes of wonderful people. I collected most of the amusements from them and from crazy people I met at other bars, clubs, and parties along the way.

The amusements in this book are not just for bartenders and servers, however. While these folks find them valuable for entertaining customers, the games are really intended for livening up parties, breaking the ice, occupying children, and impressing friends. These amusements can be used for all kinds of occasions. The best thing about most of them is that they are simple, and it doesn't take too much practice before you can perform them. As you gain experience, you'll figure out which ones work best for you. As for the more challenging ones, just practice them until you feel confident. If you mess up, just keep your cool, and laugh it off, because it's all about having fun!

All of the tricks have been rated for difficulty level:

   EASY

   A BIT TRICKY

   HARD

# FUNNY MONEY
## amusements using coins and bills

At the bar, you'll have plenty of opportunities to perform with money—and hopefully make some. One night when I was working at the Adventures Club at Disney World, a guest gave me a $1 tip folded in the shape of a bow tie. For his second drink, he tipped with a dollar folded in the shape of a ring, and, forgetting this was my tip, I left the bills on the bar. Another guest asked me about the bow tie and the ring, and without missing a beat I replied, "Oh, tonight all of my guests are folding their tips into a creation of their choice." Soon an intricately shaped collection of bills stretched all the way down the bar. The moral: These amusements will provide a starting point, but be creative and come up with some of your own and others might do the same. You never know what seemingly dull companions might come up with when sparked with a challenge!

11

# MISSING HEADS

 Here's a fun stumper to start off with. Ask someone if they can find the 14 heads on a $1 bill. If they can't, the buck is yours.

**How it's done:** 1 George head + 1 eagle head + 12 arrowheads = 14.

# KISSING COINS

OK, I admit it: For a short time I worked at Tony Roma's ("The Place for Ribs"). One day at happy hour a street-smart guy named Adam (no rib jokes, please) sat down at the bar. He said he had traveled the fair circuit for 15 years and worked the dime-throw booth. Working with so many dimes inspired Adam to come up with this amusement: Line up five coins. The challenge is to arrange the coins so that each coin is touching every other coin.

**How it's done:** It takes a very steady hand. Place two coins next to each other so their sides are touching. Lay two more coins across the first two as shown. Then wedge the fifth coin upright between the top two. The coins are all now touching.

# NORTH MEETS SOUTH

 While I was performing bar amusements one time, an adorable little red-haired girl with a southern drawl requested 10 coins so she could show me a trick. Digging into my tip jar, I handed her 10 quarters. As she began to set up the quarters, I realized I already knew the amusement, but decided to play dumb. I guess I played *too* dumb, because after we finished our bet she scooped up the $2.50 and walked away! Here's how it works: Set up 10 coins in the shape of a triangle pointing north. The challenge is to get the triangle facing south by moving only three coins.

**How it's done:** There are four rows of coins. Slide the single coin from the top row of the triangle down and around to the opposite end. Then slide the two exterior coins from the longest row up to the top row. North is now South.

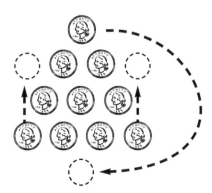

# GLASS PRISON

When you're waiting your turn to shoot pool, try out this amusement on someone. Watching them try to get the dime out from under the glass can be as much fun as banking the eight ball into a corner pocket! On top of a cloth napkin, set down a dime between two quarters. (The cloth napkin is not needed if you are using a surface covered by a tablecloth.) Balance a glass upside down on top of the quarters so it is not touching the table. The challenge is to get the dime out from under the glass without touching the coins or the glass. Blowing is not allowed.

**How it's done:** Scratch the cloth in front of the dime and the dime will slide out.

SCRATCH HERE

**Hint:** It works well to make up stories to go along with this amusement. Here are a couple I use: Face the coins heads up and say that the dime represents a prisoner, the quarters are the guards, and the glass is a jail cell. How can you help the prisoner break out of jail? Here's another example: While working in a gay club in Arizona, I said the dime represented a gay guy and the glass a closet. The challenge became helping the guy come out of the closet.

15

# HOW DOES YOUR GARDEN GROW?

Once at Disney World's Grand Floridian Beach Resort, two ladies perched at the bar, determinedly waiting for someone famous to show up. To help occupy their idle hours, I showed them this simple amusement. (Afterward, I asked them if, for my next trick, they wanted me to produce a movie star. I simply pointed directly behind them, where Chevy Chase had been sitting the entire time. They gave me a big tip!)

If you look at the tails side of a dime, you'll see two plants. Lay 10 dimes tails up and say that you bought the plants at a nursery. The person working at the nursery told you that if you plant them in your garden (set out a napkin to represent the garden) in five rows with four plants in each row, they will grow with much success. How should you plant them?

**How it's done:** Draw a five-pointed star and place a dime on each place where the lines intersect.

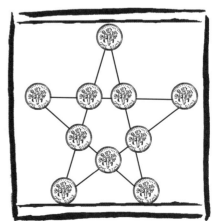

16

# THE MONEY BRIDGE

Get ready to boggle and impress with this one! (Be warned, any engineers in the group will probably figure it out.) Set out three rocks glasses and a dollar bill. Line up two of the glasses a little less than a bill's length apart and challenge someone to use the bill as a bridge on which to balance the third glass. They can only touch the bill and the third glass.

**How it's done:** Fold the bill accordion-style—making three or four creases lengthwise—to create strength. Lay the bill between the two glasses and, surprisingly, the third glass will balance on top of the bill.

17

# THE ELECTRIC COMB

If you meet a cutie at the bar and want to primp without seeming vain, this amusement is a godsend. It allows you to groom your hair and impress your new friend with your cunning all at the same time! Balance a nickel on its side and place a paper match across the top edge; then cover the nickel and match with a glass. Hand someone a comb and challenge them to knock the match off the nickel without tipping the nickel over. The person can't touch the glass with anything, including the comb.

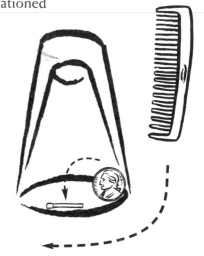

**How it's done:** Run the comb through your hair to create static electricity. Swipe the comb past the glass where the nickel and the match are stationed and the match will fall off the nickel. It's an amazing sight!

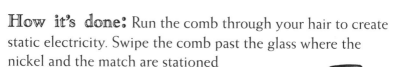

# CONNECTING PENNIES

 There was an earthquake in San Francisco and the Golden Gate Bridge split in half. Oh my! Turn a business card over and draw the broken bridge, then tape a penny on each side of the bridge to represent cars (Lincolns). The challenge is to connect the two halves of the bridge without folding, tearing, or drawing on the business card. Touching the cars is not permitted.

**How it's done:** Simply hold the business card in front of your nose and slowly bring it towards your eyes. The bridge will connect right before your eyes! Pretty cool visual, huh?

# CAGED COPPERHEADS

 My Uncle Bob first showed me this coin amusement with nine buffalo nickels (the nickels represented buffaloes). At the bar I use pennies and say they are copperheads. Draw a big square on a napkin. This represents a cage. Set the nine copperheads in the cage as shown; then challenge someone to draw two more squares inside the first cage to give each copperhead its own cage.

**How it's done:** First, draw four straight lines caging the four corner copperheads, creating a square. Then, draw another square around the middle copperhead, and all will be captured in their own cage. Pretty sssssimple, huh?

# PENNY BASKETBALL

Next time you're at your favorite sports bar and the basketball game on the big screen goes to a commercial break, play a joke on one of your friends with penny basketball. Here's how to play: Everyone sticks a penny on someone else's forehead and then passes a glass (the basket) around, hitting their chin against the bar to try to land their penny in the basket. The sucker, I mean the friend, who the joke is on bangs and bangs their head, but their penny never falls. That's a real headbanger!

**How it's done:** The penny doesn't fall because it was removed from the person's forehead. When you push a penny against someone's forehead for 10 to 15 seconds, it will stick. If you slyly remove the penny after applying pressure it will *feel* like it's there. Just make sure the bar doesn't have a mirror behind it or *you'll* be busted!

21

# DOUBLE YOUR MONEY

 My mom, Babs, showed me this one. She says every-one loves a bargain, so try to get two for the price of one as often as you can! Ask to borrow a bill and rub it on your elbow; then sing the Doublemint gum jingle, chant "double trouble" three times, or come up with your own magic spell. Rub your hands together. Open your hand, and Wow! One bill turned into two bills.

**How it's done:** Hide a crumpled dollar bill in the back of your collar. When you rub the borrowed bill on your elbow, reach naturally to the back of your collar and grab the hidden crumpled bill.

All in one motion bring it down, rub your hands together, then open your hands to show that one bill turned into two bills. Wow! Thanks, Mom! (MoM is WoW upside down, you know.)

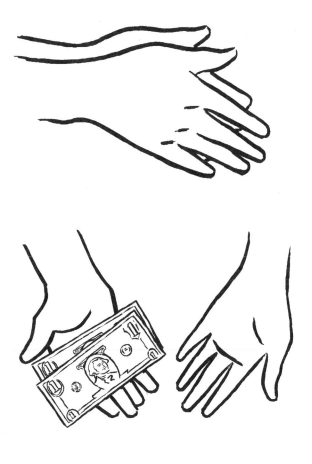

23

# HUMAN PIGGY BANK

 To produce an object out of thin air is awesome, but an equally awesome amusement is to make an object disappear into thin air. Children of all ages have an enormous appetite for this kind of entertainment and this one is very fulfilling. All you need for this trick is a coin and your arms.

**How it's done:** Say to someone that you keep all of your change in your forearm and that you're going to show how you deposit money in it. Hold a coin in your *right* hand and start rubbing it up and down on your *left* forearm. Then, on purpose, drop the coin, making an embarrassed, clumsy excuse. When you pick up the coin, pick it up with your *left* hand and only pretend to put it back in your *right* hand. With the coin hidden in your *left* hand, start rubbing your forearm again with your *right* hand, while secretly dropping the coin down your shirt.

Slowly remove your *right* hand to show that the coin has disappeared and is now in your arm. Practice this in front of a mirror a few times before trying it in front of an audience; then get ready to embrace those faces!

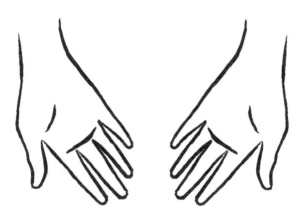

# THE LOVE OF MONEY

 At a popular military pub called the Red White & Blue in New Ulm, Germany, a bartender named Sabine (pronounced Sabina) loved American coins. She would wager to buy the entire pub a drink with this coin amusement. Sabine would scatter some of her American coin collection on the bar and then turn around. She would then ask someone to turn over five coins, one at a time, while saying "turn" out loud each time. When finished, she would ask the person to slide one coin away from the others and cover it with their hand. She'd then turn around, wave her hand over the coins, look deeply in the person's eyes, and guess if the coin under their hand was heads or tails. She nailed it every time!

**How it's done:** Before you turn around the first time, count the number of coins that are heads up and remember it. Each time you hear the person say "turn," add one to your remembered number. Let's say the final number in your head is an *even* number. When you turn around, secretly count the number of heads up coins. If there is an *even* number of heads up coins, then the coin under the hand will be *tails*. If there is an *odd* number of heads up coins, then the coin under the hand will be *heads*. It works the other way too. If the final number in your head is *odd* and there are an *odd* number of heads up coins, the coin under the hand will be *tails*. If there are an *even* number of heads up coins, then the coin under the hand will be *heads*. It might sound confusing at first, but try it by yourself a few times and you'll soon see why Sabine never bought the house a round of drinks.

# ORANGE CRUSH

Are you ready for a totally awesome amusement that will catapult you into a higher tax bracket? Here's the illusion: You borrow a bill and ask the person to sign their name on it. Roll it up, then put it in a bar towel, handing the bar towel containing the borrowed bill to someone to hold. Place a champagne bucket containing three oranges on the bar and pull the oranges out one by one, setting them on the bar. Have someone choose an orange; lay the bar towel over the chosen orange, then throw the bar towel up in the air to show that the bill is gone. Where's the bill, you ask? Inside the orange, of course! Don't believe it? Cut the orange in half to reveal a bill inside. A little juicy, but it's the *real* signed bill, nonetheless!

**How it's done:** To prep for this trick, you'll need to make a small hole in an orange, big enough for a rolled bill to fit inside. (A pen or pencil stuck in it overnight works really well.) You might have to experiment with this ahead of time to get the effect you're after. (At the end of the trick, it will have a better effect if the hole looks as natural as possible.) Next, prep the bar towel with a rolled bill hidden in the hem and set three oranges (one of them is the prepped one) in a champagne bucket. Make sure the prepped orange is sitting with the hole up.

Now you're ready for the trick: Tell your audience that you have a new trick to try and that you need to borrow a $1,000 bill. (This should get a few giggles.) Next, ask for a $100 bill, and keep decreasing the amount until you finally get someone to lend you a $1 bill. (This light-hearted patter works really well.) Next, hand the person a pen and ask them to please sign their name on the bill. Take the bill, roll it up tightly and pretend to put it in a bar towel, then hand the bar towel to someone to hold. (What you are really doing is palming the borrowed bill and handing the towel to the person, making sure that they can feel the previously hidden bill in the towel.) With the borrowed bill in your palm, misdirect your audience's attention by asking the person holding the bar towel to verify that they can feel the borrowed bill. Immediately reach for the champagne bucket and in one smooth, fluid movement, reach in and shove the palmed borrowed bill

in the prepped orange. (Try to make it appear as if all you are doing is reaching in to get an orange.) Take out the prepped orange, making sure you set it on the bar in a way so that no one sees the hole. Continue taking the other two oranges out until all three are lined up on the bar.

Here's how you get them to pick the prepped orange: In magic terminology, this is called a force. You only make them *think* they are picking the orange you are forcing them to pick. Ask them to pick *an* orange, not *the* orange. If they happen to point to the prepped orange the first time, cool! If not, simply put the orange they pick back in the bucket. If they don't pick the right one the second time, no problem, just put their chosen orange back in the bucket and you now have the prepped orange on the bar. Take the bar towel back, lay it over the orange, throw the towel up and away behind the bar, then announce that the borrowed bill is now inside the orange. Your audience will have looks of disbelief on their faces. It's now time to grab a knife, cut the orange in half, and astonish everyone when they see the rolled bill inside the orange. Take it out and let the person you borrowed the bill from verify that it is their signature on the bill. AMAZING!

30

# TRICKS WITH "STICKS"

**amusements using straws, toothpicks, and matches**

When I worked as a clown, I always carried plenty of sticks in my pockets because kids really enjoy stick amusements. As a bartender, I always have plenty of straws, toothpicks, and matches on hand, and I discovered that grown-ups love these tricks too. Hence my theory that kids and drinking adults are on just about the same mental wavelength.

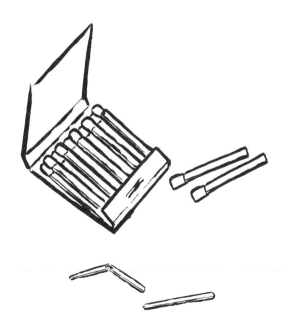

# HOUSE OF STICKS

 A good stick amusement to start off with is the House of Sticks. Don't worry, there's no Big Bad Wolf involved! Use 11 toothpicks to build a house facing east, as shown. The challenge is to get the house to face west by moving only one stick.

**How it's done:** Move the angled stick that is inside the roof to angle the opposite way and the house will be facing west.

# HOUND DOG

Listening to some blues one night at Big Dog's Still & Grill in Myrtle Beach, a bartender with puppy dog eyes showed me this dog stick trick. (I modified it by adding a bone.) You'll need 14 sticks. With 13 sticks make a dog stick figure as shown. Point out that the last stick is the dog's bone. Move the bone from the front of the dog to the back of the dog and challenge someone to get the dog to face his bone by only moving two sticks. The tail must remain up and you can't move the bone.

Arf! Arf!

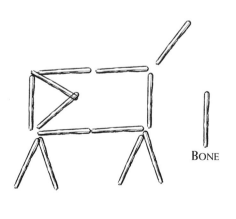

BONE

**How it's done:** Turn the dog's head to look at his bone by moving the two face sticks to the inside of his stick body.

BONE

33

# RUBIK'S CUBE

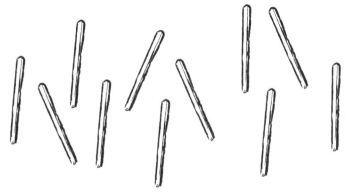 Here's one from the deceptively simple department: Challenge someone to arrange eleven sticks to make eleven squares. If they've been drinking, this could be a virtual Rubik's Cube!

**How it's done:** Make two connecting squares using seven of the sticks. With the remaining four sticks put plus signs inside the two squares. Three big squares plus eight small squares equals eleven squares.

# TRIANGLE CHALLENGE

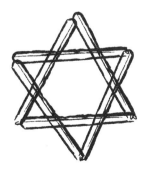 This is a great stick amusement that I learned from a bartender named Matt. It's guaranteed to keep someone baffled for at least ten minutes, so it's a great way to distract an unwanted bar Romeo or buy yourself some time on a really bad date. Lay out six sticks. The challenge is to make eight triangles.

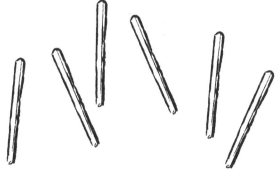

**How it's done:** Make the symbol known as the Star of David by overlapping two triangles, one pointing up, the other down.

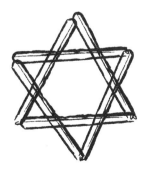

# FIVE PLUS SIX EQUALS ONE

 The Thai women I worked with on one cruise ship would often ask funny yet intelligent questions about the English language, like "What is love on the rocks and how is it different from scotch on the rocks?" "What is super duper?" "Why is the first number in the English language spelled ONE yet pronounced WON?" I think this stick trick confused them even more: Lay out 11 sticks and separate them into two groups, with five sticks in one group and six in the other group. The challenge is to arrange all the sticks to prove that five plus six equals one.

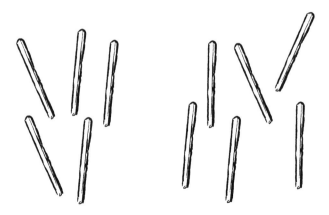

**How it's done:** Arrange them so they spell the word "ONE."

# WISHING UPON A STAR

Thank your lucky stars for this really special stick amusement! I've seen it presented several ways, but this one that I made up works really well for a birthday. Take five toothpicks; break them in half (not all the way, so they're still connected), and arrange them as shown. With a glass of water nearby, wet the end of a straw and drop a little water on the broken ends of the toothpicks. The toothpick arrangement will slowly and incredibly turn into a star right before your very eyes! For a birthday, I tell the person to think of a wish every time I drop a bead of water. Then I sing, "When you wish upon a star, makes no difference who you are, anything your heart desires will come to you." If you time it just right, by the time you are finished singing, the star will be formed.

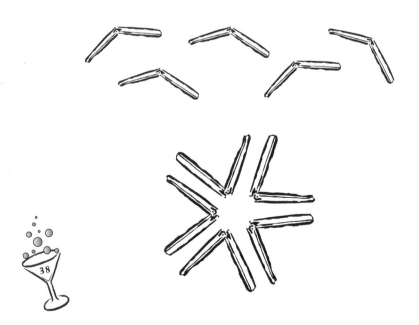

**How it's done:** When wood gets wet, it swells. By dropping a bead of water onto the broken ends of the toothpicks, the toothpicks begin to move back into their original shape, and the points of the stars are formed. May all your wishes come true!

ADD WATER TO CORNERS

# THE MEMPHIS MYSTERY

Down the street from The Pyramid (a huge replica of an Egyptian pyramid that is used for concerts and sporting events in Memphis) there is a great cook-your-own steak restaurant called the Butcher Shop. Always looking for a new bar amusement, I asked the bartender, Connie, if she knew any bar tricks. She reached over and grabbed six toothpicks and challenged me to make a Memphis landmark. With the challenge, I tried to spell out "Elvis," make a duck from the Peabody Hotel, but nothing worked. Then, Connie gave me a hint: Make four triangles out of the six sticks and that will be your answer.

**How it's done:** Take three of the sticks and form a flat triangle on the bar. Place the remaining three sticks vertically to form a 3-D pyramid shape over the flat triangle, then walk like an Egyptian!

**Hint:** You can also ask someone to create one of the wonders of the world using only six toothpicks.

# Mental Matchbooks

Are you feeling a little telepathic today? Then mystify your friends using matchbooks from the bar. Here's what to do: Lay out three matchbooks, turn your back, and ask someone to open one of the matchbooks and remove a match from it. When you turn around feel the matchbooks, then boldly announce which one is missing the match. How do you do it, oh wise one?

**How it's done:** Before laying the matchbooks out, push the flaps tightly in, to lock them in place. When you turn around and pick up the matchbooks simply feel for the one with the loosened flap and you'll know which book they opened.

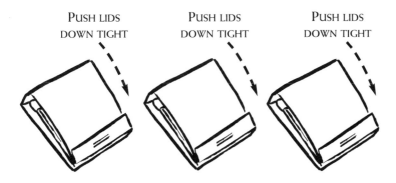

PUSH LIDS
DOWN TIGHT

PUSH LIDS
DOWN TIGHT

PUSH LIDS
DOWN TIGHT

**Hint:** Another way to present this is to pretend you are weighing them in your hands, stating that you can feel which book is lighter.

# THE UNBREAKABLE TOOTHPICK

An ex-tennis-player-turned-exotic-animal-trainer-turned-bartender named Lori tricked me with this awesome stick amusement. You don't have to be nearly as talented as Lori to master it. Lay out a bar towel and place a toothpick in the center. Fold the towel and ask someone to feel the toothpick through the towel, then ask them to break the toothpick in half. Open the bar towel and the toothpick will be intact! This amusement works really well because the person can feel the toothpick break in their hands and can't believe it when they see that it is still in one piece.

**How it's done:** Prep the bar towel by hiding a secret toothpick in the hem. When you hand the person the towel-wrapped toothpick to break, you are really handing them the secret toothpick. Be sure to fold the towel up well, keeping your finger on the hidden toothpick as you do, so that you're sure when handing it over that the hidden toothpick is what's on top and facing them when they go to break it.

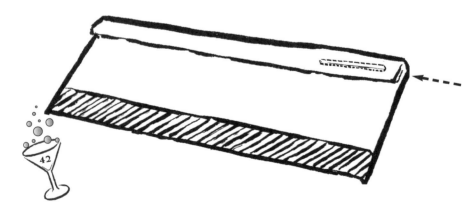

Fold napkin so that the hidden toothpick is on top—bring the left side over to the right, and fold the bottom up to the top.

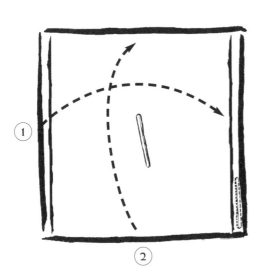

Secret toothpick

Toothpick to be broken

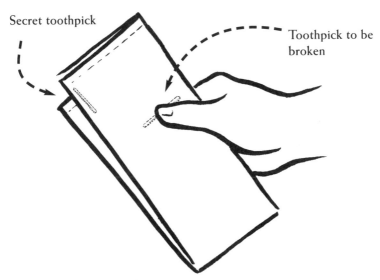

**Hint**: You can substitute a wooden match for the toothpick, or use a napkin instead of a bar towel (cloth napkins work well because they have hems).

43

# JAWBREAKER

 Here's a jaw-dropping stick amusement that my sister, Charlie, showed me. She can take a straw and shove it up through her chin. To prove this, she opens up her mouth to reveal that the straw has gone all the way inside her mouth!

**How it's done:** Beforehand, she cuts off a piece of straw that she hides under her tongue. Then she positions another whole straw under her chin, sliding her hands up to give the illusion that it's the straw that's moving. (By using her hands to cover the end of the straw, the straw appears to get shorter.) She then opens her mouth to reveal the prepped straw sticking up through her mouth, producing a jaw-dropping reaction from her audience. It takes just a little bit of practice in front of a mirror to get it down, but it's worth it!

# THE KEY TO SOBRIETY

This is a great crowd-pleasing trick! I learned it in a bar near Texas A&M (Aggiesville) and often use it as a sobriety test. Here's the setup: Take two matches from a box of wooden matches and ask someone for their car key (take it off the ring). Slip the hole of the key over one match and lean the other match against the first one, on top of the key as shown. Here's the challenge: Get the key without the balanced match falling and they can have another drink.

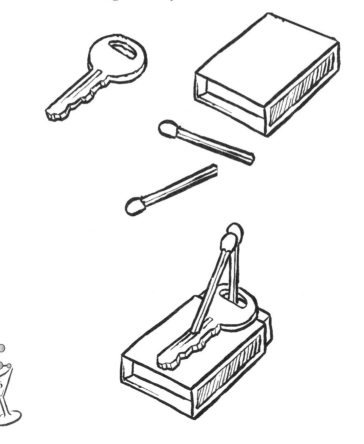

46

**How it's done:** Light the middle of the balanced match; it will burn up to the head and then fuse together with the head of the other match. When you see the balanced match curl up off the key, gently blow the flame out. You can now get the key because the balanced match can't fall.

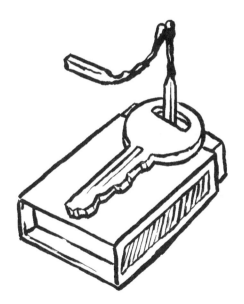

# MAGICAL MATCHES

Once I spent the day with an 83-year-old magician named Pete, looking at pictures and listening to stories about Vaudeville. He showed me this stick trick that I now use all the time; all you need is a matchbook. Here's what it looks like: Open a book of matches and ask someone to pull out a match of their choice. Close the book, ask for the match they chose, light it, and then blow it out. Lay the book of matches in their palm, make the burnt match disappear, then announce that their match has returned to the inside of the matchbook. Ask them to open the book and watch their eyes light up when they see their chosen match inside!

**How it's done:** There are two things you must do before performing this trick. First, you have to light a match and blow it out because this is the match that you are going to pass off as their chosen match. Next, you'll have to learn a magic disappearing technique called the French Drop: Hold the match between the tips of your thumb and index finger, creating a little match bridge. With your other hand, move your free thumb *under* the match bridge and close your fingers over the match pretending to grab it, but really you are dropping the match to the floor or your lap. (Practice this in front of a mirror.)

FRENCH DROP

Now you are ready to perform the trick. This is what you do: Open a matchbook with the prepped match hidden under your thumb. Have someone choose and pull out a match. As you close the book, slide the prepped match up into the book. Close the flap, pushing tightly to lock it. (You want to make sure the hidden match doesn't fall out.) Now take their match, light it, blow it out, and set the book in their palm. Perform the French Drop using their match and immediately create a diversion by bringing the hand that they *think* the match is in closer to them so that their attention is diverted there. After the match has dropped, bring that hand up to meet the other hand, say some magic words or whatever feels comfortable to you, tap the match book, show your empty hands, and tell them that their match has jumped back into the matchbook. When you see the look of disbelief on their face, ask them to open the book to see if their match is inside and magically, it is.

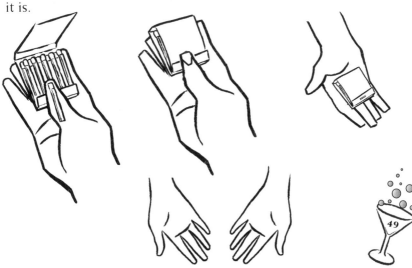

# READING ASHES

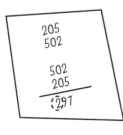 I learned this one from a bartender named Mark at a singles-pick-up-meat-market bar (you know the type) in Coos Bay, Oregon. I guess he figured out that I wasn't there to be picked up, so instead he picked up a book of matches and performed this stick trick for me. Here's what he did: First, he slid a napkin my way and handed me a pen, asking me to write down three numbers in my social security number, license plate, or any other personal number. Then he asked me to reverse the numbers, subtract the smaller one from the larger one, then circle the first number in the answer. He then reached over and took a book of matches, handed them to me and asked me (as he turned around) to tear out the number of matches that I circled, put them in a napkin, wad up the napkin, and hide it in my hand. When I was finished he turned around, took the book of matches, tore some out, dropped them into a shaker tin, set the book on fire, dropped it into the shaker, swirled it around, blew the flame out, and rolled the burnt matches out on the bar as if he were rolling dice from a dice cup. Then he studied the ashes, and amazingly announced the number of matches in my hand. He was right! Now, that's a hot little match trick.

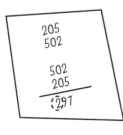

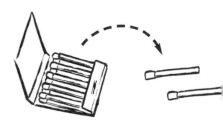

**How it's done:** All new matchbooks come with 20 matches. Before the trick, take two matches out and set the prepped book aside. After someone tears out their matches, all you have to do is tear out nine matches (but don't bring attention to the number of matches you're tearing out, you want it to seem random). Quickly count the remaining matches and mentally subtract that number from nine. This will give you the number of matches in their hand. Work up your own cool presentation, or use the one above to make an impression, as it did on me.

Hint: If you use the shaker tin presentation, you'll need to use a bar towel to handle the hot tin.

# BOTTOMS UP!

## amusements using bar glasses

Rocks, pilsner, snifter, pony. I may not know all my state capitals, but I do know my bar glasses! I've always loved 'em! Not only do they hold yummy concoctions, they are also part of a symbolic ritual: the toast. We raise our glasses in unison and clink them together as if to say, "So be it!" (Or as *Star Trek's* Captain Picard would say, "Make it so!") You'll have tons of fun performing these glass amusements, and as you do, here's a toast: When life hands you lemons, reach for the tequila and salt!

# A GLASS ACT

This first amusement is fun because most people figure it out fairly easily, and that makes them feel good. It's a great one to warm up your audience. Set up six glasses in a row, with liquid in the first three. The challenge is to get the glasses to alternate (empty, full, empty, full, empty, full) by moving only one glass.

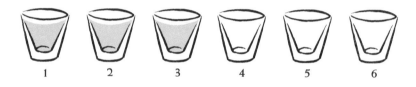

**How it's done:** Pick up glass #2 and pour the contents into glass #5. Now the glasses alternate.

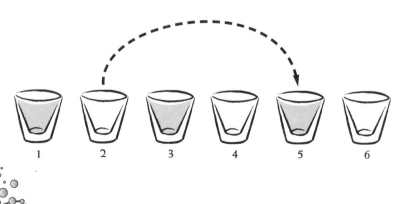

# MIDNIGHT AT THE OASIS

Here's an amusement I made up myself. When you run into someone who smokes Camel cigarettes, set up four clear glasses of water (two glasses back-to-back on the left and two glasses back-to-back on the right). Place the pack of Camels in the middle between the two sets of glasses. Tell this story: The camel on the cigarette pack has been in the desert for a long time and is getting thirsty. He is also getting very confused and thinks this water (point to the glasses the camel is facing) is an oasis—but it's not. It's just a mirage. The water over here (point to the other set of glasses) is the oasis. If the camel is facing the mirage, how can you turn him around so that he faces the oasis, without touching any of the glasses, turning the pack, or moving the pack past the glasses?

MIRAGE          OASIS

**How it's done:** Whenever you put an image behind two glasses of water, the image appears in reverse. So just slide the camel behind the glasses on the left. Look through the water—you've turned him around!

55

# THE FLYING LIME

At a wonderful artsy restaurant and bar called Café TU TU Tango in Orlando, my best friend, River, and I watched a bartender hold a drink behind his back, then throw a lime over his shoulder, catching the lime on the edge of the glass. He did this all night long and never once did he miss. Now that's some juicy talent!

**How it's done:** He never missed because he had stuck a lime on the edge of the glass before putting it behind his back. His talent turned sour when we noticed all the limes on the floor.

56

# THE FLOATING FIFTY

One night a very rude man sat at the end of the bar. He never tipped all night long. Not once did I give him the satisfaction of getting a reaction out of me. At the end of the night he yelled goodnight to me and I smiled and waved as if he were the biggest tipper in the world. Later, when I went to clean up the area where he had been sitting, I found that he had left me a $50 bill floating in a glass of water. Wait, it gets better: The glass of water was upside down on the bar!

**How it's done:** He stuck the bill in the glass of water, set a coaster on top of the glass, carefully turned it over onto the bar, then slipped the coaster out. Just make sure you have a bar towel handy to retrieve the cash!

# HOT SHOT

You don't have to visit Italy to learn that Sambuca will catch fire. Next time you or someone else orders this yummy licorice shot, challenge them to pick up the shot of Sambuca using only their flat palm.

**How it's done:** First, wash your hands (please) and leave the palm area a little damp (this will prevent the flame from burning you). Light the shot, then cover the glass with your flat palm; the oxygen will burn, creating a suction. Now carefully lift your hand, making sure to keep your palm flat or you'll lose the suction. Salute! (Pronounced "sah-lood.") That's Italian for cheers!

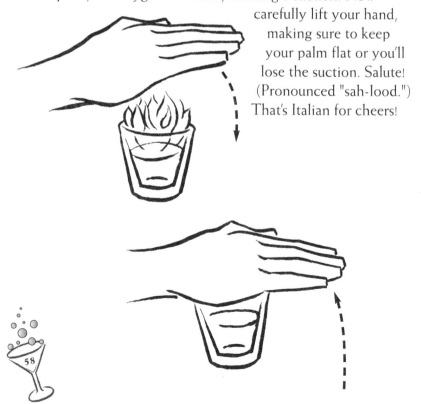

58

# TIPSY WINO

If you've ever wanted to be popular, then get ready to capture a lot of attention with this wine glass amusement. Hold a glass of wine on a table and tilt the glass. Slowly remove your hands to leave the wine glass balancing on its own. It's a stunning sight, provided no one bumps the table!

**How it's done:** With a little help from a wooden match or round toothpick secretly planted underneath the table-cloth, you can tilt and balance a glass of wine that is one-third full. Rest the bottom edge of the glass over the hidden match. Gently hold the tilted glass, slightly adjusting it as needed, until you can slowly release your hands. Practice this a few times in advance to get the feel of it, and add some slow magician-like hand sweeps around the glass for drama. A cloth napkin works too, if a tablecloth isn't available.

HIDDEN TOOTHPICK

# LIQUID RAINBOW

If you're interested in skyrocketing your tips behind the bar, this is a fantastic glass amusement to get you started. When two or more people order a round of shooters, mix the shooters, line the glasses up, then pour. What's so spectacular about that, you ask? Each shooter you pour comes out a different color!

**How it's done:** Food coloring. Secretly prep some glasses with a drop of food coloring in the bottom of the glass. Talk them into a relatively clear shooter like a Kamikaze or Lemon Drop for the trick to work best. And don't worry about them seeing the drop of food coloring; just keep the glasses close to you. (In all the times I've performed this, not once did anyone ever see the drops.)

# THE JUMPING EGG

The next amusement reminds me of a pretty nurse named Angie. She never could do the trick quite right, but she kept the bar entertained all night long! Set up two shot glasses side-by-side and put a whole egg (raw or hard-boiled) into one of the shot glasses. Ask someone to move the egg into the other glass, without touching the egg or either glass. Nine times out of 10, they will ask you to repeat the rules.

**How it's done:** Blow hard into the air pocket of the shot glass and the egg will jump over into the other glass.

Blow

**Hint:** This trick can be an incredible crowd-pleaser. Never start off with this one. Always work your way up to it for the best effect.

# A Very, Very Dry Martini

 If you're giving a swanky party and someone asks, snootily, for a very dry martini, give them a dry martini—literally. Here's how it works: Pour liquor into a shaker, add ice, attach the strainer, and swirl. Sounds normal, right? But not when you tip the shaker to pour the drink into a martini glass and nothing comes out! That's what I call a very dry martini.

**How it's done:** Prep the shaker by lining the bottom with napkins to absorb the liquor. (I usually fill an empty gin or vodka bottle with water ahead of time and pour that instead—using the real stuff isn't particularly cost effective!)

**Hint:** You can substitute other drinks and liquors to your imagination's content.

# GLASS WEDGY

I learned this trick in Seattle from a police officer named Verita. It goes beyond the expected and requires some finesse, so try it at home before trying to impress your date! Set two straight-sided glasses upside down. Put money under one, then balance a wooden match in between the glasses, making sure that the match head is touching the empty glass. The challenge is to remove the money from under the glass without letting the match fall.

**How it's done:** Light the match head using another match and wait two seconds, then blow out the match. (You have to use a white-tipped, "strike anywhere" match. You can find them at your local grocery store.) Continue to gently blow on the match, allowing it to cool and fuse to the glass. You can now slide the empty glass over and collect your money from under the other glass.

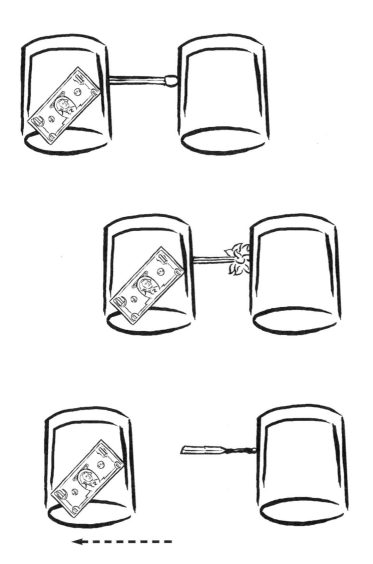

**Hint**: For fun or to torment someone, you can place a variety of items under the glass. I have used this amusement as a sobriety test and have challenged someone to get car keys out from under the glass. Once when I was asked for my phone number, I wrote it on a napkin and stuck it under the glass. Be creative! Be naughty!

# TOWER OF GLASS

This next amusement wins hands down for scaring the most people. They tend to back up a little, but are too interested to go far. You'll need three matching glasses and two pencils. (If you happen to have only pens at the bar, then wrap a beverage napkin around two pens.) Set up the first glass with the two pencils laying opposite each other on the rim of the glass. Next, hold the other two glasses rim-to-rim under water, allowing both glasses to fill up. (Make sure the rims are touching—and remain touching—when they come out of the water.) Lift up and let the excess water on the outside of the glasses drip off. Holding the glasses together, set them on top of the pencils. Here's the challenge: Get the water in the top (upside down) glass into the empty glass on the bottom without touching anything.

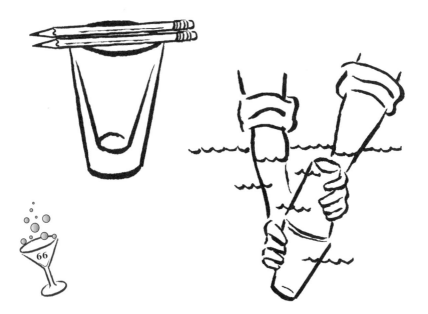

66

**How it's done:** With a small cocktail straw, find the air pocket between the two rims and gently blow. Believe it or not, the water from the top glass will dribble down and fill the bottom glass. The most memorable time I performed this one was on a cruise ship for John Phillips of the Mamas and the Papas. (The ship swayed a little, almost upsetting the precariously balanced glasses, and the look on his face was priceless!)

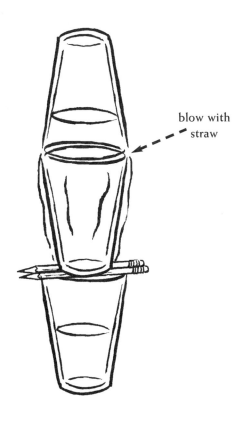

blow with straw

# The Cherry Challenge

 Here it is: The first bar amusement I learned, and it's a crowd pleaser. You'll need a brandy snifter, a stemless cherry (rinsed and dried), and a glass of any kind. Place the snifter upside-down over the cherry. Challenge someone to get the cherry into the glass without touching the glass or the cherry. The only thing they can touch is the snifter, and the only thing the cherry can touch is the snifter. The snifter must remain inverted at all times. (Mashing the cherry on the rim is not permitted.)

68

**How it's done:** Centrifugal force, of course! (See, you should've paid more attention in physics class!) Holding the base of the glass, rotate the snifter around and around in circles until the cherry spins around the inner rim. Lift the snifter off the table and all the way over to the glass; when you slow the rotation, the cherry will drop into the glass.

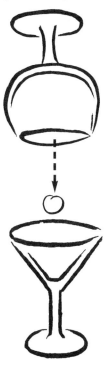

**Hint:** For dramatic effect, try these: Make hurdles using bar items for the cherry to travel over; drop the cherry into a Manhattan; substitute an olive for the cherry and drop it into a martini; or drop a cocktail onion into a gibson (if you have good aim).

# 99 BOTTLES OF BEER ON THE WALL

**amusements using beer, wine, and liquor bottles**

There are more amusements you can do with a bottle other than blowing across the top to make a whistle—although that little number can sometimes entertain a buzzed barfly for hours! You will amaze and astound even somewhat sober folks with these bottle amusements, and maybe even make a few bucks. If there's one prop that's abundant in bars, it's bottles. Make use of 'em!

# LONG-NECK MONEYMAKER

 Here's an example of a classic bottle amusement that I first learned at Michigan State from a bartender named Sherry. It can be a real moneymaker. Turn an empty bottle (preferably long-neck) upside down on top of any bill. The challenge is to get the bill out from underneath the bottle without knocking over the bottle. You cannot touch the bottle, and it must remain inverted at all times. Of course, if you succeed, the bill is yours.

**How it's done:** Roll up the bill until it pushes off the bottle.

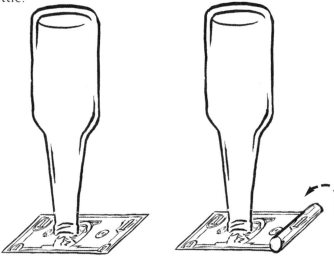

**Hint:** The first thing people will think of is to pull the bill quickly out from underneath the bottle. This will work on slick surfaces, unless you make sure the bill gets a little damp where it meets the bottle. The few drops of beer left in the bottle can help you out here.

# Bottle Pick-Me-Up

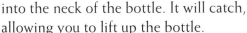 Were you the reigning neighborhood champion of games like pick-up sticks and Operation as a kid? Then you might be a natural for this one. Set out a bottle and a straw. Challenge someone to pick up the bottle using only the straw. Wrapping the straw around the bottle is not permitted.

**How it's done:** Bend the end of the straw and insert it into the neck of the bottle. It will catch, allowing you to lift up the bottle.

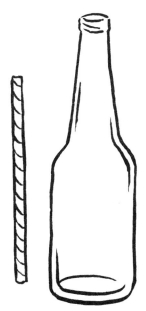

73

# BOTTLE DROP

 Hangin' out in O'Blarney's in Lacey, Washington, a patron named Ken stumped the table with this bottle amusement. He dropped a straw in a bottle, then challenged us to get the straw out without tipping or touching the bottle.

**How it's done:** He poured water in the bottle and the straw rose up and out of the bottle.

# Bottomless Bottle of Wine

My favorite wine bottle amusement is to wait until a bottle has been sipped, savored, or even chugged, then challenge the consumers to drink one more shot from the empty bottle.

**How it's done:** Turn the empty bottle upside down, pour some liquid into the indention on the bottom, and drink. You drank another shot from the bottle!

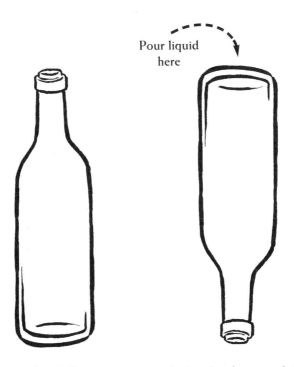

Pour liquid here

**Hint:** You can also challenge someone to drink a shot from a sealed bottle the same way.

# IT'S YOUR DIME

A great follow-up with the empty wine bottle is to set a business card on the mouth with a dime on top of the card directly over the opening of the bottle. The challenge is to get the dime into the bottle and the rules are that you can only use one finger.

**How it's done:** Flick the business card and the dime will lose its center of gravity, allowing it to fall straight down into the bottle. Practice this a couple of times to get the feel of the flicking.

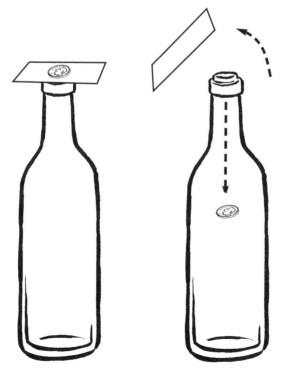

# GENIE IN A BOTTLE

Continuing with the previous wine bottle amusement, with a dime inside an empty bottle, cork the bottle and challenge someone to get the dime out of the bottle without removing the cork or breaking the bottle.

**How it's done:** Anyone who has had the experience of having a bottle of wine but no corkscrew should know the answer to this one: You have to push the cork into the bottle.

77

# THE CORK CHALLENGE

 The dime is out of the wine bottle and now you are stuck with a cork inside. Might as well challenge someone to get the cork out (without using the bottle to christen anything, of course).

**How it's done:** Work a cloth napkin or scarf into the bottle to capture the cork. Slowly pull the napkin out and the cork will come with it.

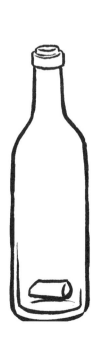

78

# BOTTLED BEER ON TAP

 A bartender at the Jack Daniel's Saloon at the Opryland Hotel in Nashville challenged me to get some beer out of my bottle without tipping it over or using a straw.

**How it's done:** First, the bottle has to be full. With a quick and solid tap on the top of your bottle from the bottom of another full one, the beer will rise and foam, causing it to come out of the bottle. Have your mouth ready!

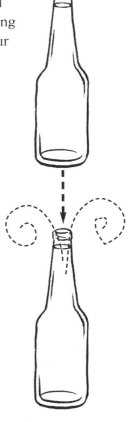

79

# BEER
# CHUG-A-LUG

 Some college boys from Iowa State showed me how to chug a bottle of beer faster than anyone. You can even give your opponent a head start by allowing them to drink half of their beer first!

**How it's done:** Insert a bent straw in the bottle, bend it out of your way, and chug. The straw allows air flow and the beer will stream out of the bottle.

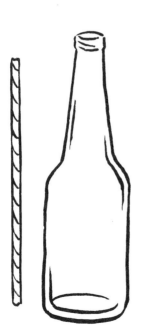

**Hint:** For the quickest airflow, a "bendy" straw works best.

# BAR BLAST BOTTLE ROCKET

If you can't make it to Cape Canaveral to watch a shuttle soar to the sky, then make your own bottle rocket at the bar!

**How it's done:** Make the rocket with a straw and a toothpick inserted crosswise a quarter of the way down the straw. Take an empty bottle of 151 and heat it up by running very hot tap water on it. Insert the rocket with the toothpick at the lip to hold the straw. Start counting down; light a match, drop it in, and watch out! The 151 left in the bottle will burn up, pushing the rocket straight out of the bottle. Blast off!

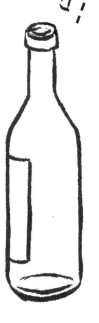

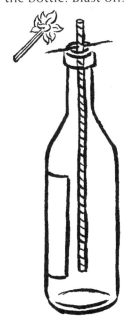

81

# DEAD SOLDIERS

If you're working behind the bar or throwing a big party, you can accumulate a lot of wine bottles. Make use of them and perform a mind-blowing bottle amusement that will certainly entertain your winos, I mean friends. Here's how it works: Set five empty wine bottles in a row on the bar, with the corks stuck in them. Add a full bottle of wine to the end of the row so there are now six, then ask for a volunteer to go across the room and turn their back. Ask your friends to pick one of the empty bottles and pour just a little bit of wine from the full bottle into the chosen empty bottle. When finished, send the full bottle across the room and just by smelling the wine, the volunteer will be able to tell which empty bottle had wine poured into it, without turning around.

**How it's done:** You and the volunteer are in on the trick together. Before the trick, mark the tops of the corks. One pen dot for bottle number one, two pen dots for bottle number two, and so on. (Just make sure you set them out in order.) Don't worry, no one will see the tiny dots. When the group pours a little wine into the chosen empty bottle, all you have

to do is switch the corks, making sure you put the marked cork in the full bottle of wine that will be sent over. All the volunteer has to do is look at the top of the cork, add a little play-acting as if they are a real connoisseur of wine, and you'll have a mind-boggling bottle amusement.

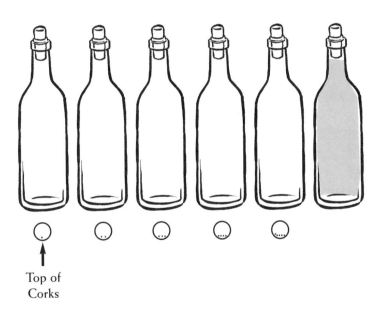

Top of
Corks

# SWING, BOTTLE, SWING

In the U.S. Virgin Islands on the island of St. Thomas, there's a man-made beach called Magan's Bay. It is beautiful! At the palm-thatched outdoor bar, a bartender had a Cruzan Rum bottle hanging from a string. No, the bottle had not committed suicide; it was a prop for a freaky bar amusement. I asked the bartender to show me this unique bottle amusement, and he began to swing the bottle back and forth, from side to side. The challenge is to get the bottle to swing in a circle, without touching it or blowing on it.

**How it's done:** The trick is to have a pair of polarized sunglasses nearby. Keeping both eyes open, hold a lens over only one eye. The bottle will *appear* to be swinging in a circle now! Change eyes and the bottle circles in the other direction. Freaky! Especially when you've been drinking rum all day!

# THE FLOATING COCKTAIL

Teaching bar tricks at Walt Disney World gave me the opportunity to meet other instructors who were teaching their favorite style of bartending. There was lots of flair (bottle-flipping) to be learned, but a guy named Todd blew fire. He was awesome! His act demanded full attention, and believe me, he got it. So much, in fact, that Vegas snatched him up from Disney so he could perform his show-stopping fire act there. Before he left for Vegas, he told me about this awesome bottle amusement to add to my collection: Hold a glass in your hand, pick up a liquor bottle, then pour some into the glass. Sounds normal, right? Here's the awesome part: Take your hand away from the glass and it will float in mid-air as liquor is still pouring into the glass.

**How it's done:** This is a totally prepped trick. Here's what you'll need: strong fishing line, a treble hook (it's the one with three hooks on the end—make sure to cut off the sharp points), a fishing weight, a safety pin, a lighter, a plastic glass (that's an oxymoron, isn't it?), a dark liquor bottle, a pourer, and some brewed tea (to look like liquor). Prep the plastic glass by making two tiny holes on each side, so that you can tie a piece of fishing line across the inside of the glass. To make the holes, light the point of a safety pin and while it's still hot, burn a tiny hole through the glass as shown.

85

TOP VIEW OF CUP

Run the fishing line through both holes, and tie a knot on one end so it doesn't fall out.

To prep the bottle, start by tying a second piece of fishing line to the hook; then thread the line through the pourer, and attach the weight on the end, allowing the line to drop about half-way down into the bottle. Pour some tea into the bottle, snap the pourer on, and you're ready to go. Attach the hook to the fishing line inside of the glass and begin pouring with the bottle close to the rim of the glass so the line can't be seen.

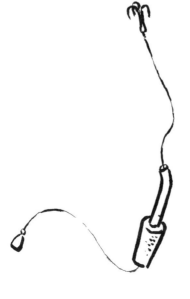

86

Once the liquid begins streaming out, raise the bottle until the line to the glass is taut, then let go. The glass will appear to be floating. Make sure you practice this and when you perform it, it's best to have a crowd because it's a real show-stopping amusement that no one is soon to forget!

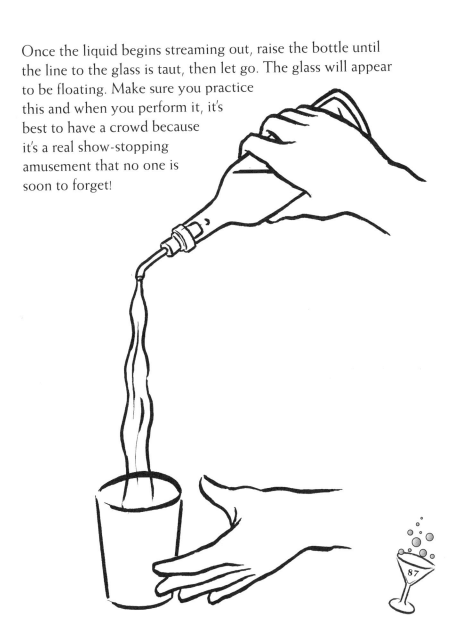

# PAPER TRAIL

**amusements using paper and pen**

Pen and paper amusements were probably some of the first amusements we learned as children. Who doesn't remember playing countless hours of hangman or tic-tac-toe? Well, you're all grown up now, but you can still relive those fine memories at the bar.

# BAR DOODLES

Here are some great warm-up pen and paper amusements to break the ice, get a smile, or just lighten the mood. I picked them up from a bartender at the Bamboo in Kissimee, Florida. I love these things!

## What is it?

1. A man who got his bow tie stuck in an elevator.
2. Looking down on a person wearing a sombrero frying an egg.
3. A tomato sandwich.
4. A nun with headphones on.
5. A bubble-gum-blowing champion.

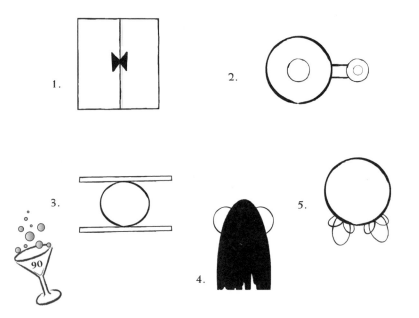

90

# THE CHAIN

Aretha Franklin sings about the chain chain chain of fools, but if you can figure out this paper and pen amusement, then you ain't no fool! Here's what to draw: Draw 15 circles in three-link sections to make five chains as shown. The challenge is to figure out the least amount of cuts you'd have to make to connect all the links together into one big chain.

**How it's done:** Two cuts (as shown).

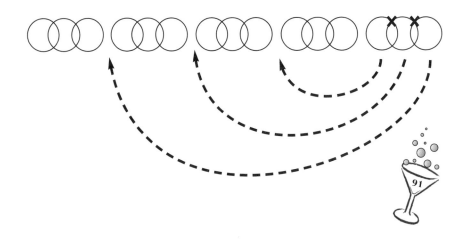

# THE CIRCLE OF LIFE

Now, let's aim for a target. Grab a napkin and draw a circle with a dot in the middle and challenge someone to make that same drawing without taking their pen (or pencil) off the napkin.

**How it's done:** Fold a corner of the napkin up to the middle. With your pen, make a dot; then gradually unfold the napkin back to a square while still keeping the pen on the tip of the folded corner. Now begin to draw the circle. See, not once did you take the pen off the napkin! Better wager a drink on this one.

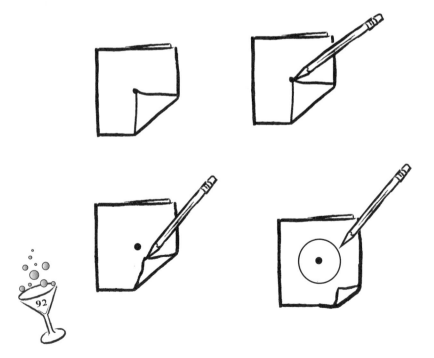

# SPORTS WITHOUT BALLS?

Okay, I admit it. I am not a sports fan. But a lot of people out there are fanatics, so I make sure I have some sports amusements in my collection. Guys are very competitive and can be easily led into a friendly wagering game to see who buys the next round. Here's what to do: Divide some guys (and gals) into two groups. Hand each group a pen and napkin, asking them to write the numbers one through eight. The challenge is to answer this question: List eight sports that do not have the word "ball" in them. The first team finished with the correct answers wins!

**How it's done:** Tennis, golf, rugby, soccer, ping pong, billiards, bowling, croquet, squash, swimming, diving, skiing, gymnastics, track & field, badminton, horseback riding, cricket...

# WHEN IN ROME

 A bartender at the Galveston Hilton in Texas got me with this pen and paper amusement. He drew the Roman numeral for eleven (XI) on a napkin and challenged me to draw one continuous line to make six.

XI

**How it's done:** Turn the napkin upside down and draw the letter "S" to make SIX.

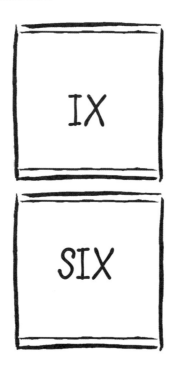

IX

SIX

# NINE DOT
## CONNECTION

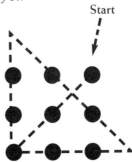 While working on a ship, a bartender named Melissa showed me this paper amusement. She's a wonderful artist, and says that everyone can draw dots and lines, so challenge someone to connect nine dots (in three rows of three dots each) with one continuous line. The line can only cross each dot once.

**How it's done:** Start your line at the upper right-hand dot and connect diagonally to the lower left-hand dot. Then go straight up to the upper left-hand dot, and continue past it, as if there were another dot just above it. Draw another diagonal line through the middle dot of the first row and the third dot of the second row, continuing past it as if there were another dot to the right of the last one in the bottom row. Extend the final part of the line through the last two dots that haven't been connected yet.

Start

95

# The Coaster Challenge

Put on your thinking cap and write the numbers one through seven on seven coasters. The challenge is to arrange them in a way so that they add up to 12, horizontally, vertically, and diagonally.

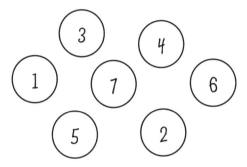

**How it's done:** Arrange the coasters in three rows. In the first row, place the numbers 6, 1, and 5. In the second row, place the 4 directly under the 1. In the third row, place the 3, 7, and 2.

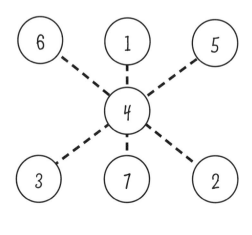

96

# COCKTAIL NAPKIN CROSSWORD

 If you love crossword puzzles and no one left a newspaper at the bar for you, then this pen and paper amusement is for you! All you need are nine cocktail napkins with these letters written on them: T, Y, P, G, I, A, E, E, and C. Your challenge is to arrange them so that there are six three-letter words spelled across and down.

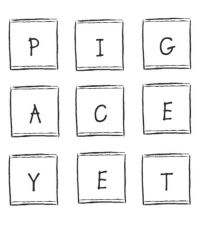

**How it's done:** You will have three rows of three. The words reading across are PIG, ACE, and YET. The words reading down are PAY, ICE, and GET.

| P | I | G |
|---|---|---|
| A | C | E |
| Y | E | T |

# A COMMON INTEREST

 Rick, one of my favorite bartenders, showed me this one. Write these two phrases on a cocktail napkin: ENID AND NADINE, LIVE NOT ON EVIL. The challenge is to figure out what they have in common.

ENID AND NADINE

LIVE NOT ON EVIL

**How it's done:** They both spell the same thing forwards and backwards.

# WHAT'S UP, DOC?

I don't know this for a fact, but I would lay down money to bet this would be Bugs Bunny's favorite amusement. Here's what you do: Take a napkin and write the word "carrot" on it; then fold it and stick it under a glass. After asking a series of short questions, nine times out of ten you can get someone to say "carrot." Then ask the person to look at the word you predicted and placed under the glass.

**How it's done:** Very quickly and without hesitation ask: What is 9+1? 8+2? 7+3? 6+4? 5+5? 4+6? 3+7? 2+8? 1+9? Name a vegetable. (Urge them to say the first vegetable that comes in their head; it's almost always "carrot.") Try it!

# CRACKING THE CODE

 Did you ever dream of being a secret agent or private investigator when you were a kid? Finding secret messages and collecting clues? Then this paper and pen amusement was designed for you! Here's what to do: On five cocktail napkins write the letter sequence as shown. The challenge is to decipher the message, and find out what letter goes in the center of the fifth napkin.

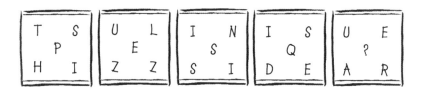

**How it's done:** Starting with the first napkin, read counterclockwise beginning with the top left corner and ending with the middle; continue on to the next napkin. When finished, you will discover that the letter you need to write is the letter "S." The code is THIS PUZZLE IS INSIDE SQUARES. Way to go, Sherlock!

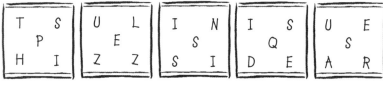

# A PERSONALITY TEST

I stepped back in time one night in a swanky little club called the Chez Nous, in Phoenix. The guy sitting next to me at the bar was a psychiatrist. (At least that's what he said.) He gave me a little test that I found astounding, and I have used it countless times at the bar for fun or to just get a quick lowdown on a person. You'll be amazed at the results! But be warned: If you really like personality tests, stop here and don't look down the page any farther; then let a friend take over so you don't ruin the outcome.

**How it's done:** There are four questions:

1. What is your favorite animal? List three adjectives that describe why.
2. What is presently your favorite color? List three adjectives that describe why.
3. What is your favorite body of water? List three adjectives that describe why.
4. You are in a dark room and you know you are going to be there for 24 hours. List three adjectives that describe how this makes you feel.

The answers in #1 represent how others see you.
The answers in #2 represent how you see yourself.
The answers in #3 represent your sexual energy.
The answers in #4 represent how you feel about death.

**Hint:** Try to get the person to take their time and answer from their heart. The test will turn out surprising results! How did you do?

101

# GRAB BAG

## amusements using an assortment of objects found around the bar

People used to try and stump me by pointing to an unlikely object and saying, "Do a trick with that!" When I would, they'd be amazed. Sometimes I'd even amaze myself! You'll find yourself thinking more creatively after doing bar tricks for a while... so you see, these even have educational value!

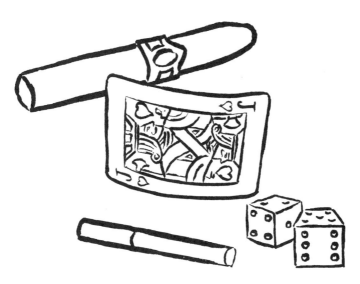

# THE SELF-LIGHTING CIGAR

Can you light a cigar by swiping it across an ordinary American dollar bill? Before the cigar craze began, I came up with the idea of hiding a wooden match inside a cigar, then lighting it by swiping the cigar across the strike plate on a box of matches. This self-lighting cigar went over really well. One day a dancer on the cruise ship showed me how to light a match by striking it across the president on an American bill. (There are little ridges on the president's jacket.) An even cooler amusement was born!

**How it's done:** You'll need to use white-tipped matches (also called "strike anywhere" matches) for this trick.

# COLD CASH NAPKINS

Would it interest you to know how to turn a napkin into cold, hard cash? If so, then grab two napkins and hand one to a sucker, I mean friend. Bet them the price of a drink that your napkin will hit the floor before their napkin will. The only rule is that you must drop the napkins at the same time.

**How it's done:** On the count of three, wad up your napkin. This will allow it to drop straight to the floor, while their napkin floats like a feather. Cha-ching!

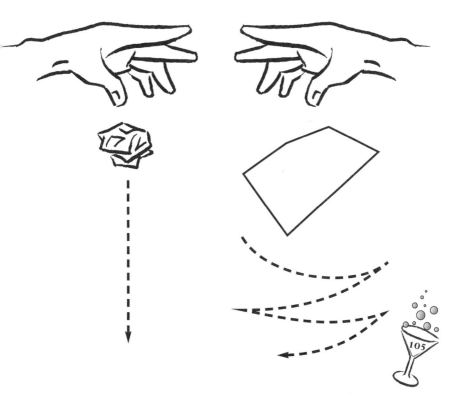

# THE FLOATING CUP

 I have found that performing humorous amusements works like a charm to lighten the mood, break the ice, or just to make someone smile. Here's one that will do the trick, as well as amaze and entertain: Hold a paper (or Styrofoam) cup between your hands, then slowly release it, allowing the cup to float in mid-air.

**How it's done:** Punch a hole in the side of the cup and stick your thumb in it. Make sure your audience is standing at the proper angle for this trick to be most effective or you'll be busted sooner than you wish. Clasp both hands around the cup, and with a very careful attitude, slowly release your fingers one by one to build up audience attention. When your hands are released, they won't see your thumb and the cup will appear to be levitating. (Take a moment and check out those faces!) After about 10 seconds, loosen up your body language and flip the cup over to reveal your thumb sticking inside of it. Adults will give a rip-roaring laugh (or at least a generous giggle) and kids will want that cup right away so they can try it. Practice in front of a mirror to get the natural feel for it. You'll find that it's really easy!

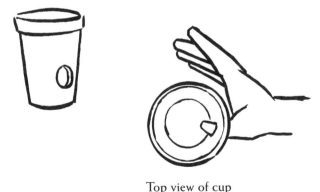

Top view of cup

Hint: I have also performed this with a beer/soda can. A root beer can is a great prop, because then you can make a root beer float!

# THE BILLIARD BETCHA

Here's one I picked up at the Barrel House in Boulder, Colorado. You can win a free beer with this one. Rack and set up a pool table as normal, then lay your cue stick across the width of the table. The challenge is to roll the cue ball (that's the white one, duh) under the cue stick.

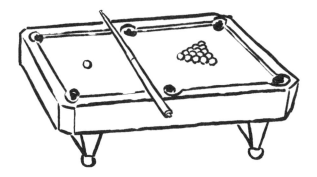

**How it's done:** Pick up the cue ball, and roll it under the table. The cue ball has now rolled under the stick. Enjoy your brew!

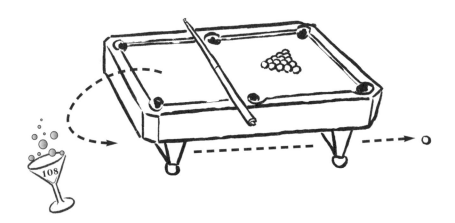

108

# CARD BALANCE

 On the cruise ship, a swinger named Jack King (for real!) came into the casino to play blackjack every day of the cruise. (Guess what he drank? What else, Jack Black!) He showed me this amusement: Challenge someone to get a playing card to balance on its side.

**How it's done:** Bow the card a little and it will stand on its side. (It's best to try this amusement with someone who's a little tipsy. They'll never think of bowing the card!)

# The Shirt Off Your Back

There you are at the bar, setting up a favorite wagering amusement, and your volunteer bets the shirt off his back! When your volunteer has lost the wager, reach over and literally pull the shirt off his back in one swift second!

**How it's done:** The trick is on everyone else at the bar because your volunteer is really your secret helper. Your volunteer will need to be wearing a jacket, coat, or a pull-over sweater and a button-down shirt underneath. Have them redress themselves (privately) without putting their arms in the shirt sleeves, draping it on like a cape. Put the jacket on, make some minor adjustments with the top of the shirt, button or zip the jacket a little to cover up where the bottom part of the shirt doesn't cover, and all looks normal. If you have a pull-over sweater, you just have to make sure the shirt collar is intact. Within earshot at the bar, casually comment about how much you like that shirt, blah, blah, blah. Then pick a wagering amusement and the fun has begun!

110

When the time comes for the volunteer to pay up, reach over and grab the shirt by the collar and pull it off their back. The looks on everyone's faces will be priceless. I guess there's more than one way to lose your shirt!

# PSYCHIC DICE

At a casino bar on Paradise Island in the Bahamas, a bartender handed me three dice and asked me to drop them in my glass of water, lift the glass up over my head, count the total of the dice on the bottom, then set my glass back down. He then dipped his finger in my water, rubbed it on his forehead, and after a little concentration announced my total. Amazingly, he was right! (But I was just concentrating on not taking a drink from my water!)

**How it's done:** Dice have this seven thing going on. All you have to do is add up the total of the numbers on top and subtract that number from 21 to know what the bottom total is. Totally!

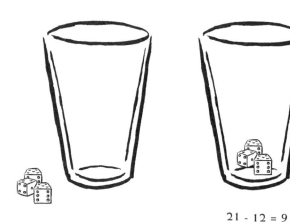

21 - 12 = 9

**Hint:** I usually just use an empty glass so they can shake up the dice. When finished, I would then set the glass on my head and pretend to concentrate, but I'm silly like that.

# NICE DICE

 A lot of bars have dice and dice cups for patrons to roll for the jukebox, a round of drinks, or just to play horses. Once when I was working at a local bar, I added a big twist to the bar's dice and cup that was such a big hit, regular customers started to bring their friends in just to watch the expressions on people's faces.

**How it's done:** I used those BIG furry dice that hang from rearview mirrors, and made a BIG dice cup from an empty Baskin Robbins ice cream container. I dressed up the dice cup with some leather-like material from the fabric store, then dropped in the dice. It was hilarious!

**Hint:** This is from experience: Take the dots off the dice and hand glue them back on or they will fall off.

# THE MONEY TREE

A server at Julia's in Montego Bay in Jamaica cut a lime in half at our table and there was a dime inside! I guess money does grow on trees there!

**How it's done:** Stick a dime on a knife using rubber cement, then make sure your audience is sitting on the opposite side where they can't see the dime. When you cut the lime, squeeze the inside of the lime against the knife to release the dime. This will give the illusion that the dime was inside the lime. Try it with lemons and oranges too! And it also works really well if you first make a dime disappear, then have it reappear in the lime. (See "Human Piggy Bank," p. 24.)

# HEAD GAME

The Baja Beach Club in Lake Buena Vista, Florida, has foam parties all the time. I always wondered if the club attracted a lot of people because of the foam, or because the waitresses wear thongs. Anyway, a bartender there would ask a group of people to secretly decide on a number between one and ten. After the number was agreed upon, he would put a little foam on his thumbs and touch each person's forehead while intently concentrating. When he was finished, he announced what the secret number was and was right every time! I guess that foam is magical.

**How it's done:** The bartender had a secret helper who clenched his teeth the number of times of the secret number.

When the bartender put his fingertips up to the secret helper's temples, he could feel the helper's temples moving and counted the number of times they moved. Now that's a real head game!

115

# CASABLANCA

"Of all the gin joints in all the towns in all the world, you had to walk into mine." While you're here, show me how to whistle with that olive left in your martini. You do know how to whistle, don't you? Just put your lips together and blow.

**How it's done:** Take the olive out of your martini (remove the pimento). Put the ends of your thumbs in the crooks of your index fingers. Place your thumbs together, bending the tops of them to make a little "V." The olive should be behind the "V." Put your lower lip on the thumb joints and blow across the upper edge of the olive. This might require a little practice to get the line-up of the olive with your blow. Maybe not today, maybe not tomorrow, but soon, and for the rest of your life...

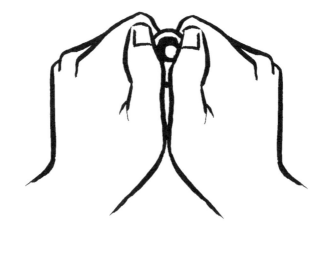

116

# LIGHT UP THE NIGHT

 At a swing club called Atlantic Dance at the Boardwalk in Walt Disney World, a bartender asked my friends and me who we would like to see perform at the club. We each gave him an answer, and he wrote each one down on a napkin, folded it up, and dropped it into a champagne bucket. Then he asked me to reach in and take out one of the napkins and secretly show it to my friends. Dropping a little 151 rum in the bucket, he set fire to the remaining napkins. He then announced what was written on our napkin, and he was right!

**How it's done:** The first answer that is given is written on every single napkin.

**Hint:** Of course, you can modify it by changing categories: sports teams, colors, movie stars, etc., and you can use a shaker tin if a champagne bucket isn't handy.

# CARD SHARK

When I worked on a riverboat in Little Rock, my boss showed me this card amusement. It's one of my favorites.

In card-trick terminology, this amusement is called a "force." In other words, you *force* the participant to pick a certain card—without them knowing it, of course. Take a deck of cards and hand it to the participant to shuffle. When they hand the deck back to you, secretly look at the card on the bottom and memorize it—then stick the deck in your pocket. Don't forget which card is on the bottom, because that's the card you are going to force them to pick.

Let's say, for example, that the bottom card is the jack of hearts. Ask the participant to name two suits. (Remember, you want them to pick hearts so you can eventually lead them to your card!) If the two suits they choose are clubs and spades, tell them that *leaves* diamonds and hearts. If they choose diamonds and hearts, simply proceed with the amusement.

Of the two suits left—diamonds and hearts, in this example—again ask the participant to pick one. If they choose diamonds, tell them that *leaves* hearts. If they choose hearts, great! You're halfway there.

Ask the participant to pick six cards in consecutive order from the suit of hearts. If cards ace through six are chosen, say that *leaves* seven through king; if cards seven through king are chosen, all the better. Next ask the participant to narrow the six cards down to three. If they say eight, nine, and ten, well, that *leaves* jack,

queen, and king. Out of jack, queen, and king, ask the participant to pick one card. The bottom line is, you're narrowing
down the deck until you force the person to choose the card
that you want them to (in this case, the jack of hearts).

When the person finally picks the forced card, tell them that
you will now reach into your pocket and pull out their card—
but would they like you to produce the card on the first,
second, or third try? (You know where the forced card is,
remember: It's the bottom one.) If they choose the second or
third try, simply pull any other card from the deck first, then
on the second (or third) try go for the jack of hearts.

# SWEET DISAPPEARANCE

I don't know if you know it or not, but sugar has a strange reaction when it comes into contact with pepper. You can actually hold a pack of sugar in your hand, sprinkle some pepper on it, and it will disappear!

**How it's done:** Of course by now you know it has to be trickery, and this one is all about misdirection. Hold a sugar packet in your fist and say that you need the pepper. As you reach over for the pepper you will bring attention to the reach, while your other hand is getting rid of the sugar packet in a pocket, your lap, or even on the floor.

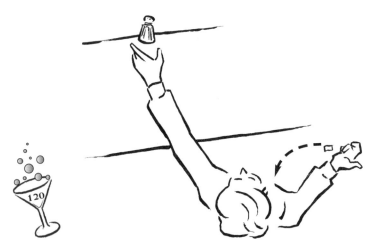

120

All while this is happening, talk about the strange reaction sugar has when coming in contact with pepper, blah, blah, blah. As you bring both hands together, one with a pepper shaker and the other close-fisted, sprinkle pepper into your fist (your audience will think that the packet of sugar is still inside your fist).

Shake your fist, and slowly open your hand to show the packet of sugar is gone. If you want, while all the attention is on the disappearing sugar, drop the pepper shaker in your lap to disappear! This little amusement will spice up your life.

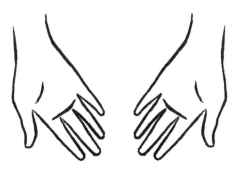

# THE POWER OF LOVE

One time our ship hit the dock in St. Thomas and we were stranded for a week. True, there are worse places to be shipwrecked. Rather than sitting thirsty on a deserted island, we spent a lot of time at a bar with a gigantic lobster on the roof, and the bartender there showed me this amusement: Put a smudge of cigarette ash on the back of someone's hand and tell them to rub the backs of their hands together until the ash is gone. Magically, you'll show them that the ash has gone through their hand and is now on their palm.

**How it's done:** Prep your middle finger before the amusement by dipping it in an ashtray. Ask someone to hold out their hand, palm down. Reach for their hand, and as you do, touch their palm with your middle finger (to secretly plant the ash). At the same time you are doing this, distract them by saying, "Oh, just bring your hand a little closer," (or higher, lower, etc.).

THIS HAND IS SECRETLY PLANTING THE ASH.

When the ash is in place, ask them to make a fist. Dip your finger in the ashtray (with them watching), and rub ash on top of the hand on which you put the secret ash.

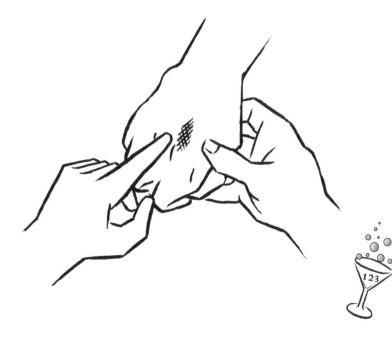

From this point on, it's up to you what you want the person to do—just as long as they keep their hand closed. For example, sometimes I ask people to do the Pee Wee Herman/Tequila dance, then ask, "Who do you love?" I tell them to declare their love for that person while rubbing the backs of their hands together until the ash is gone. When the ash has been removed, I say the power of love is so great that it has pushed the ash all the way through their hand. When they open up their hand to look, wow! The ash is now on their palm.

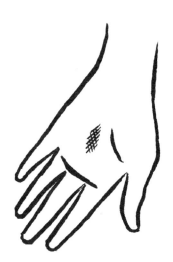

# HOT ICE

The most awesome cigarette amusement I ever saw was when a bartender at the Hard Rock Café in New York City lit a cigarette using a piece of ice. I had to barter five of my tricks and leave a generous tip to get the secret to this one!

**How it's done:** Metal potassium. When moisture touches potassium it ignites, so he had a little bit (about the size of three pin heads) hidden by some loose tobacco in the end of the cigarette. When he brought the wet piece of ice to the end of the cigarette, it ignited.

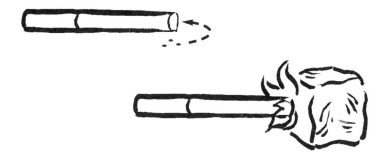

**Hint:** You can find metal potassium by looking in the Yellow Pages under "chemicals" and then calling chemical companies. It can be *very* dangerous and can even ignite from the moisture in the air. So be *very* careful if you attempt this amusement! Metal potassium is stored in glass jars filled with mineral oil and will come either in grounds (my favorite) or sticks. The smallest amount they usually sell is 10 grams, which should cost around $250. Unless you need a lifetime supply of the stuff, get some friends to go in on it with you and get ready to turn up the heat with this spectacular bar amusement!

# ALPHABETICAL INDEX

# INDEX
# BY DIFFICULTY

# EASY

# A BIT TRICKY

135

# HARD

# ABOUT THE AUTHOR

Cheryl Charming has devoted a large part of her life—almost 20 years—to entertaining barflies. After growing up in Little Rock, Arkansas, with a penchant for travel, she parlayed her restaurant and bartending experience into a job on a cruise ship, where she quickly established herself as resident expert in tricks, riddles, and magic. She found she loved amusing people, and they loved sharing their own tricks with her . . . the best of which she began jotting down on cocktail napkins, until her collection reached several hundred. A natural performer, Cheryl watched her tips get larger and her customers have more fun thanks to her playful tricks—and many friendships were formed with passengers whom she then visited around the world, collecting bar tricks along the way.

After five years on the cruise circuit, Cheryl began dividing her time between the ship and bartending at the Grand Floridian Beach Resort, the most exclusive place to stay at Disney World. She soon began teaching a mandatory magic trick course for all Disney servers and bartenders so that more people could join in the fun.

In addition to her bartending career, Cheryl has traveled extensively, studied art, and worked as a clown for 10 years doing parades, parties, balloon sculpture, magic, and storytelling. A resident of Florida, she finds herself ready to open her cache of bar tricks from around the globe, in hopes that amateurs everywhere can share the pleasure of watching someone's face light up by way of a simple trick at the bar.

What's wrong? Not enough bar amusements to quench your thirst? Then ride those cool electric waves and surf on over to Miss Charming's Free Bar Tricks at

**www.charmingbartricks.com.**

(No lifeguard on duty.)

Need a little more information on a trick in this book? Maybe you have a comment or two? Or maybe you won the lotto and want to share it with Miss Charming... Yeah, that's the ticket. She can be reached at

**cheryl@charmingbartricks.com.**